An Assortment of Poetry
By Sky Boivin

Other Books By Sky Boivin

An Assortment of Poetry
Scattered Emotions
Inspired Thoughts
Random Thoughts
Something Loved
Their Hope Within The Flames

Copyright
Sky Boivin august 26, 2013

Me For Me

Grow old along with me,
and in time you will see,
just what this life
has done to me.
The wrinkles around my eyes
and mouth show all the smiles
in all my days.
The graying hair,
shows all the wisdom
I have acquired.
Look into my eyes,
and behold the sorrows
of my life.
The hardships in my hands
and feet.
But, that is only the outside.
Try opening the window
into my soul.
I just might let you
see me for me.

                    Oct. 19, 1998

Rose of a Princess

Sweet, kind princess.
What has happened?
Something horrible,
I'm afraid.
For a strong and caring lady;
Loved by many
and all;
has died a terrible death.
The shock
of the car crash,
stunned the world.
Now, the news
of her death.
So early in age.
So tragic,
Shocking and disbelieving
To the entire world.
So much sorrow.
So much talk about it.
The world cares;
And is coming together,
in peace and sorrow.
The palace is drowning,
in a sea of flowers.
For the death of
The beloved Princess Diana.
     Sept. 5, 1997

One Night

The sky was such a pretty blue,
with a shade of green kissing that and the horizon.
The first few stars were just starting
to make their appearance to the world again,
as night fell upon the land here in Boylston.
And as a plane was flying overhead,
I saw perfectly clear, something larger and brighter go
over the plane.
A shooting star perchance?
Most likely so.
It was going so much more faster than the plane.
It was falling away from the
school in such a sudden white light,
passing beneath the trees and then fading into the
cold, winter night, forever.

Jan. 8, 1997

4.18.2013

Like a skyscraper Boston will prevail.
They will overcome.
They will come out on top and above this tragic event.
The community is reconnecting together even across the country.
The community is looking for closure.
Baseball teams are playing
"Sweet Caroline" at their games,
to show their love and sorrow to Boston.
Banners flying on stadiums
With our most beloved rivals logo and ours reading
"united we stand".
Flags at half-mast across the state.
A community waiting on closure.
A father whose son lost so young in life.
Wife and daughter still being tended to
in the hospital.
Now word on a branch of church
coming to Boston?
To Protest??
Protest What??
Having a service for the little boy so his family,
And the community can have just a slight amount of peace?
To be together and grieve??
How can't they see that what they are thinking is wrong?

Hello, Goodbye

Hello, wherever you are.
It's just me, feeling this feeling again.
Wondering how all three of you are.
Why did you have to leave me?
So quickly, and suddenly?
Without any forewarning about the
December cold approaching you.
I did not have the chance to
Say all that I had wanted to say.
I am not sure how to put it now.
But, I shall just sum it up right here and now:
I love you all.
And I miss you.
Love forever,
but never good-bye.

      Nov. 18, 1996

Grotesque Faces

As I lie awake in my bed,
I stare up towards my window.
My dried silver dollar plants
are up by my window.
The moon strikes
the plants in such a way,
that they take on shapes.
They become faces in the moonlight.
But not just any faces.
They are horror and grotesque faces from all over the world.
They are screaming
in agonizing pain.
They seem to be screaming
For help.
But for what? From what?
Are they lost souls
Which have been entangled
and trapped within these plants? Do they want to be let out?
What horrors have they encountered
while they have been trapped
within these plants?
What type of a plant
could these be?

Who could have done this?
How has it become possible, for a plant of such divine
Splendor be able to
capture and torment
Lost souls in such a
Horrific and indescribable way?

        June 13, 1997

My Cat Moon

My cat moon up so high,
Night after night, you open your eyes wider
upon the world. What do you
See? I wonder
what pleasures of the evening
do you witness and discover?
Will you let me in, on the secrets?
Or do I discover them, myself?

My cat moon, sleek and sly, up high in the midnight sky.
Dolphin-shaped cloud, soaring by.
What do you see, my black cat?
Up high above the world?
I see you, but, do you really see me?

Soar

I wish I was a bird.
Soaring wild and free.
Free from the stress and
Pressures of the world.
Free from violence,
Free from fear.
I wish I was an eagle.
Flying high above
The world.
Flying with the clouds.
Soaring just above the lakes.
Without a care for the
Threats of everyday living.
To be at peace with the world,
To be a bird,
Soaring wild and free.
Yes, that would be
A sight to see.

    March 18 1997

On the Ledge

I seem to be drawn to this place.
It calls to me.
And I go to it.
The ledges beckon me to sit
on them. As though, they are
lonely, and miss the
company from the past.
To go over there,
To sit,
To think.
And I will.
Yes, someday soon I will sit
and think on those ledges.
Just like those
From years past.
And I will be
Just like them.

June 9, 1997

Summer Slumber

Long after a thunder shower
On a summer-like day,
The mist that had settled
Around the ground,
Still lingers there.
And there is a wave of mist
rising up from the tree tops.
On my right is the setting sun.
The world is covered in mist.
And the red eight o'clock setting sun,
Seems to be engulfed by it,
As if the mist is hungry for light.
The sky, of what is seen,
Is a pale blue.
The clouds are an array
Of pink, rose, orange, and peach.
A beautiful contrast
To go along with the fire-red
Setting summer-like sun.
And with the moon to my left,
Playing hide'n'seek with the
Gray rain clouds.
And as the cool evening draws nearer,
the world grows quieter.
And into a slumber of
Summer rest.

June 13, 1997

Time

I wish I could turn time back, I wish it
did not happen.
If I could, I would,
go back in time
to stop it from happening.
To stop an innocent girl from dying,
to stop my dear friend's pain,
For the loss of her best friend

Nov. 10, 1995

The Stranger and the Light

To sow a seed,
to plant a thought,
thoughts and
visions and dreams
become one
in my mind.

I dream of
peace, love, and
happiness and
I hope that
those I shall
find someday.

If not today
then maybe
tomorrow.

If not tomorrow,
then maybe soon.
If not by myself,
then maybe
someone else will
find them for me.

To find my
visions that I
have within
my mind,

I find them all
hidden within
my dreams when
I sleep.

When I sleep,
I go down
deserted roads
and hallways.
All by myself.
But sometimes
I'm not alone.
There is a
stranger.

A stranger
travelling beside
me.
It is dark so
I cannot see
this stranger.

I do not know
who this stranger is.
This stranger
travelling beside
me.

Sometimes, it seems
as if there
is a light ahead.
A light which
maybe filled
with wonderful
splendors.

I try to travel towards
that light,
for maybe it
holds the answers
to some of my
Questions.

Questions that
no one else knows
the answer to.
I keep travelling
towards the light.
But something is
holding me back.

I do not know
Who or what that
Is holding me away
From this light.

Dying To Be Free

So many thoughts keep racing
Through my mind.
My head is in a spinning frenzy.
Ideas are becoming
More tied together,
More complex;
As the days tick by.
I have not picked up
This sacred pen for so long
I know that it is not
That I have forgotten how.
A true artist never forgets
Life is just flying by.
Slowing my time for freedom.
To reach my pen
To my paper. But now,
My mind, body, and soul are screaming at me.
Ideas are swooning.
All is crying to be let out.
I must free it all.
I must let it go.
Grab my sacred and precious pen.
Reach for my paper.

Let me ignore
All around me.
Let me alone.
So that I may open my mind,
Heart, and soul.
So that I may
Let the words flow from my mind;
Through my arm,
Fingers;
Through my pen
Upon my paper;
To let these feelings
Dying to be
And crying
To be free
From hiding
And confinement.

                                        April 25, 2000

Boundaries

It seems that all my life
I've been chasing after the sun.
And until now,
I've been getting nowhere.
Just when I was about to quit,
You came around the bend.
You reminded me not to give up.
I was trapped within boundaries
That could not be broken.
You opened the doors
And let me be free.
You showed me the way again.
Once, I knew.
But crazy life made me forget
The things I loved.
You reminded me to be me.
Thank you for bringing
The world back to me.

Jan. 23, 2001

Life

Sinking ball of orange fire
Within the sea of clouds.
Hiding behind this grand city.
You who is coloring the world.
You who paints the clouds,
Pinks, roses, purples, oranges, and more.
You who is readying for night.
Along with the rest of us.
Stuck in traffic,
I stare past the red light
Into your orange fire.
Admiring the colors you've created
The sky is an ever-changing canvas
That bends and shapes
At your will.
How I wish life was just
As easy as that looked.
But, maybe for you,
It's not as easy as it seems,
But only gets better with practice.

Jan. 23, 2001

American Love

My world as I know it,
will never be the same.
I sat at home
watching the screen,
as the planes pierced the Twin Towers,
making them crumble.
[my world is being attacked].
Mom got a call at 3:30:
George is okay.
To my ears, the horror;
The Pentagon as well.
[Is my cousin okay?]
America will not sit around
and let terrorists scare us.
We are united as one.
[we shall stand strong].
Everywhere you look,
Red, White, and Blue proudly worn.
Let the good old
American Love Shine Through.

                              Sept. 14, 2001

Canvas of the Sky

The sky is one big Canvas.
Where there Is a certain someone,
That paints clouds Into the sky.
Many times a day.
Changing their appearance.
They make them big and small.
They make them white and puffy,
Soft and lumbering
Over us in the sky.
At sunrise and sunset,
They paint the clouds
In an array of colors.
In peach, pink, purple.
In orange, apricot, rose.
In many other shades
That we may see
When we look up at the sky.
So the next time
You look up at the sky,
Try to imagine what this
Someone may look like.
This someone whose
Canvas is the sky.
Painting clouds for us to see.

July 19, 1997

TAREHI Forever

Departing times is drawing
Closer everyday.
Old friends and new friends
Are soon to be departed.
But the memories of our past-
The good and the bad,
Will continue to live within us.
We will always remember pep rallies
And assemblies, Getting out of classes.
And the field trips,
Though few a year, if any,
And always a blast.
Our class and friends are one of a kind.
That is what has made us who we are.
Everywhere we go,
Everything we do.
We always come back with
Memories for the future.
And as we go on our separate ways,
We will bring with us,
Our memories of our high school life.
And many years after,
We will look back upon
Our memories and recollect

All the times we have shared.
TRHS class of 1997-
You will always live in my heart forever.

                                          Love always

                                          May 14, 1997

Destination Unknown

I feel like taking a trip
To some outrageous place.
Some new place to explore and discover.
And maybe even rediscover
Other things that I have forgotten.
But just where would I go?
Oh the possibilities!
There are so many places
In existence that we can go.
Hurry! Pack your bags,
Before I change my mind.
We'll run away to a
Destination unknown
And let this crazy world
Go on its busy way
Without getting in ours.
We'll leave a note
For those who care,
We'll return when it's over.

Feb. 19, 2001

Clouds

Trees bare from
their spring-time leaves and gray-old bark,
worn with time.
A pale pink-white
Behind them,
And leading heaven-way. White-blue,
Transforming into
A richer pale blue
Until it kisses the clouds.
Closer clouds are pure white.
The further away,
The darker and
Brighter at the same time.
The morning sun
Is hiding behind them.
The wet ground
Is beginning to dry now.
And the wind blows perfectly.
Not too hard nor too subtle. Imagine,
waking afresh in the morning.
But walking out
Onto the beach instead.
Standing at the shore, In a windbreaker.
Staring out onto the sea.
Inhaling the sweet perfume
Of the salt and sea. Dreaming,

Wondering,
What awaits out there. Dreaming away,
The wind ruffles at my pages.
All I see is QCC campus.
The people walking
Here and there in the sunlight
That is trying to melt
Through the clouds.
I wonder how my Dear friend is doing,
And when she will get here.

        12.4.1998

Return to the Mist

The mist welcomes me.
Wraps around me in a cool, crisp, hug.
The mist is thick upon the pond.
It beckons to me,
Thick and mysterious.
I can almost see the old boat
Guided by the swamp people.
Do I dare go to the water's edge?
Are they looking for me?
Do I dare stand along the water
And call for that boat?
Will the goddess to send them to me?
'come to the water's edge, I am here.'
Do I dare climb into the boat
Guided by the swamp people?
Do I dare see if I can part the mist?
'will she think I am ready?'
Or will I be shut out forever,
Never to see Avalon again.
'your Morgaine is here.
I am ready to return home Lady.
If that be your will.'
The mist is so thick I breath in
The cool crisp air surrounding me.
Alas no boat comes to the shore.
She is not ready to receive her Morgaine Le Fay as of yet.
I still have more to learn.
Alas, I continue to wait for the day
I can return to the mist.

5.10.2013

Boston Strong

Just a regular holiday.
That's how it started out, until a bomb went off.
Three killed
And many more innocent people injured.
Others still run around to help.
The entire community pulling together
And staying strong throughout it all.
Worldwide showing their love
and compassion because of what happened.
Photos posted on television-
"look out for these two suspects."
Parts of the state on lockdown for almost a day.
One dead and the other in custody.
Oh how the tide has turned for them.
We will overcome
those who seek us harm.
And we seek justice to right the wrong.
We will unite strongly to help everyone
To Stand again
To Walk again
To RUN a marathon again.
And we do this because we are
BOSTON STRONG.

4.25.2013

<u>July 17, 1997</u>

with the summer morning sun
coming up in the early morning hours,
The sunlight gently streams
down to the ground through
spaces between the trees.
And the moisture and wetness
upon the ground,
adds a touch of natural beauty
to the world.
Another day.
A new day.
One that will be different.
One with new possibilities.
One filled with hope.
One filled with everything,
that a new day may hold.

Death Road

The early morning hours,
Cruising down the road.
Waiting for the light to change.
Turning down the road.
Driving to work.
Continuously scanning the street in front of me.
A white cross,
Nailed to a tree.
Symbolizing the death of someone.
The body of a small raccoon.
Lying on the side of the road.
Unmoving to the living world.
A few days later,
Another creature is there.
A small puppy dog.
They go too fast on that road.
Too much death and pain
Is bought about
On Death Road.

                              Sept. 24, 1997

The Outcasts

What is an "outcast"?
Everyone should know that.
The high school clichés and groups,
The "cool", the "nerds",
The "hackers", the "athletics",
And of course,
The "outcasts".
What makes up the "outcasts"?
It's everyone else
Left out of the other groups.
They have no one place to go.
So they hang together.
Everyone else thinks
That the "outcasts"
Will be the ones out on the street,
When in reality ,
Who is it that rules the world?
The "outcasts"
Because they're smarter and tougher.
They're united as one.
From the very beginning.
The "outcasts" are really
The "geniuses" of the world!

Made in the USA
Columbia, SC
09 June 2018